Engraved by Samuel Sartain, Phil'a

Yours affectionately
Wm. S. Higgins.

In Memoriam William S. Huggins.

THREE SERMONS TO YOUNG MEN,

PREACHED BY

REV. WILLIAM S. HUGGINS,

OF KALAMAZOO, MICHIGAN,

AND A

FUNERAL DISCOURSE,

BY REV. SAMUEL HASKELL.

WITH

AN ACCOUNT OF THE FUNERAL AND MEMORIAL MEETING.

PHILADELPHIA:
PRESBYTERIAN PUBLICATION COMMITTEE.
1862.

HENRY B. ASHMEAD, BOOK AND JOB PRINTER,
Nos. 1102 and 1104 Sansom Street.

To the Memory

OF THE

REVEREND WILLIAM SIDNEY HUGGINS,

THE DEVOTED PASTOR, THE ACTIVE CITIZEN, THE FAITHFUL FRIEND, THE CHRISTIAN SCHOLAR, AND THE WISE COUNSELOR OF YOUTH,

THIS VOLUME IS AFFECTIONATELY INSCRIBED

BY THE

YOUNG MEN OF HIS CHURCH AND CONGREGATION.

CONTENTS.

INTRODUCTION.

This little volume is the result of an effort on the part of the Young Men of the church and congregation of Rev. Wm. S. Huggins to do honor to his memory, and, in some measure, to perpetuate his usefulness. A sense of duty that cannot be escaped, not less than the spontaneous suggestions of their hearts, impel them to this publication. While others mourn him as the faithful, devoted Pastor, the tried and true friend, the public-spirited citizen, or the accomplished scholar, they sorrow for him most deeply as the friend to young men. He had not himself so long passed the period of youth as to lose his sympathies with and interest in this large class of the community. To them were ever open the treasures of his richly-stored library, or of his yet more richly-stored mind; with them he conversed freely on the great themes of Christian theology and life, in the Sabbath-School, at their places of business, in the domestic and social circle—literally obeying the Divine command, "As ye go, preach;" for them he prayed and labored much, and in their behalf the last energies of his valuable life were expended. The great vacancy left by his death will never for them be wholly filled. Their language is:

> "Gone before us, O our brother,
> To the spirit-land;
> Vainly look we for another,
> In thy place to stand."

It seemed fitting, then, that the series of Sermons written for their temporal and eternal welfare, and whose composition and delivery, it is now known, drew heavily upon his failing strength, should receive publication at their hands. It is all that is left to them now of duty to their beloved Pastor—in this and other suitable ways to hallow his memory, and preserve it to posterity. But the Memorial Volume, the monumental marble towering above his sleeping dust, or the eulogies that have been spoken in his honor, cannot so perpetuate his usefulness as the teachings of his life—the inculcations from his pulpit, the words of wisdom which he spoke, whose results, it may be hoped, are enduring as the ages of eternity.

"Servant of God, well done!
 Rest from thy loved employ;
The battle fought, the victory won,
 Enter thy Master's joy.

"The pains of death are past,
 Labor and sorrow cease;
And life's long warfare closed at last,
 His soul is found in peace.

"Soldier of Christ, well done!
 Praise be thy new employ;
And while eternal ages run,
 Rest in thy Saviour's joy."

Of the three Sermons to Young Men, published in this volume, the first has already appeared in print, the second was repeated at the urgent request of many of his congregation, and the third is the last sermon written and delivered by the Pastor. Two other discourses were given in the series—one an address delivered on a funeral occasion some years ago, and the other a sermon pronounced at the ordination of Rev. MARTIN POST, of Schoolcraft, Michigan, in February, 1862. As they were not prepared especially for the purposes of young men, and were not among the latest efforts of his life, it has not been thought well to insert them.

In the hope and with the prayer that the publication of these discourses, with the matter appended, may be effectual in perpetuating the memory of a wise and good man, and be blessed to the salvation of many young men, wherever they may go, this volume is now committed to the public.

Kalamazoo, Mich., May 31*st*, 1862.

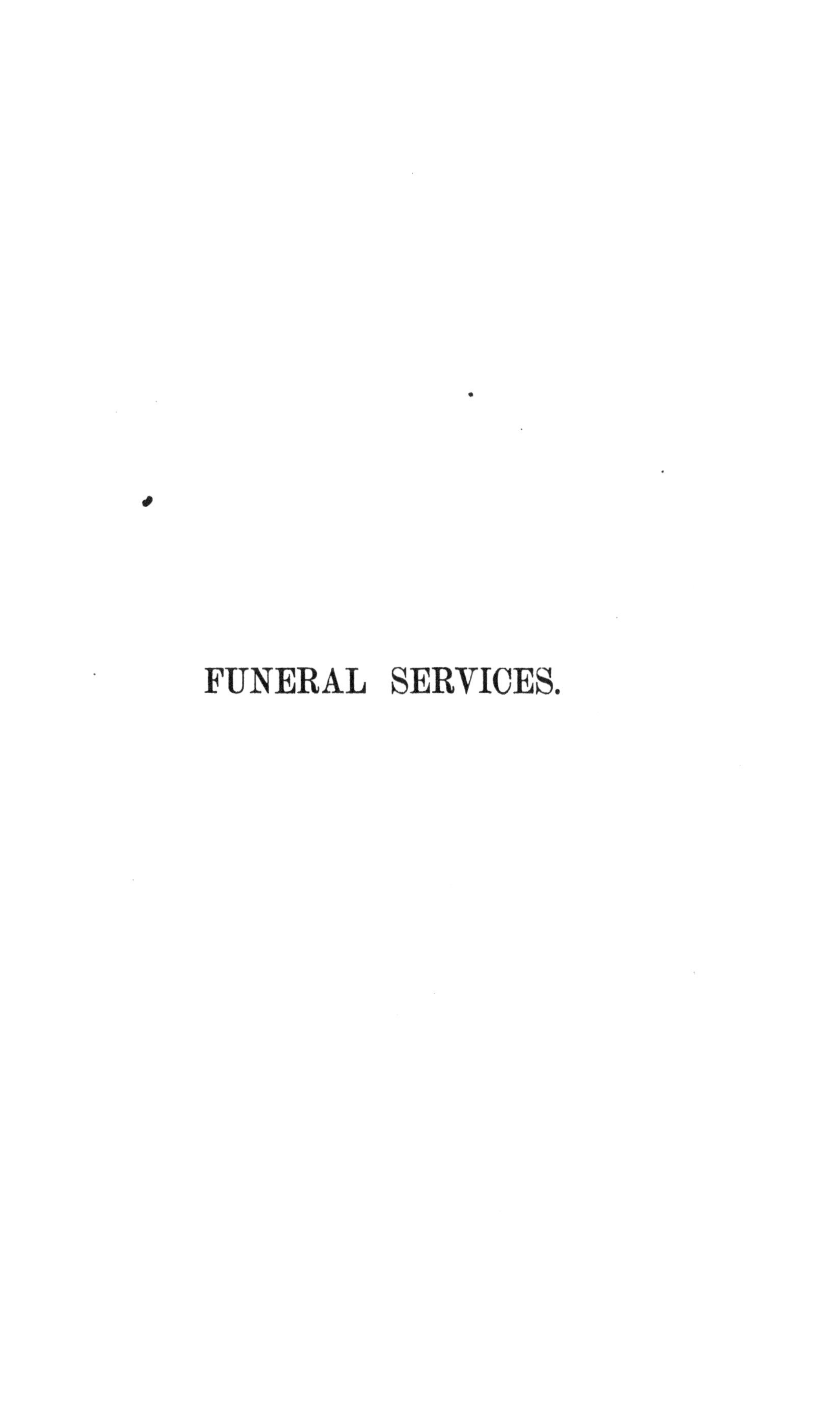

FUNERAL SERVICES.

THE FUNERAL SERVICES.

[From the Kalamazoo Gazette, March 28th, 1862.]

THE funeral services of Rev. W. S. HUGGINS were held in the Presbyterian Church, on Wednesday afternoon, (26th inst.,) at 1½ o'clock. The spacious building was densely crowded, and many left unable to obtain a place. Nearly a thousand persons were present. Among them were Hon. E. C. WALKER, of Detroit, an intimate friend and classmate of the deceased; Rev. O. P. HOYT, of Elkhart, Ind., formerly Pastor of the Church; Rev. Messrs. CHAPIN, of Ann Arbor, McCORKLE, of Marshall, BRYANT, of Niles, BARTLE, of Decatur, DAVIES, of Battle Creek, GASTON, of Hastings, BRADLEY, of Richland, APTHORP, of Cooper, POST, of Schoolcraft, and others from abroad. The clergy of the village, who were to conduct the exercises, alone occupied the pulpit.

At the appointed hour, the remains of the lamented dead, deposited in a splendid metallic coffin, inscribed with his name, age, and date of death, and covered with a rich pall, upon which were laid a crown of laurel, a cross of evergreen, and a wreath of immortelles, were borne through the door by

2

which the living form was accustomed to enter the sanctuary from his study. The following gentlemen served as pall-bearers:

Henry Gilbert,	F. E. Woodward,
Alfred Thomas,	Alfred Wilson,
I. D. Bixby,	John D. Rice,
C. W. Hall,	D. O. Roberts.

Rev. Geo. Willard, (Presbyterian,) opened the exercises by a solemn invocation, and continued them by giving out the hymn, entitled

THE PASTOR'S DEATH.*

Rest from thy labor, rest—
  Soul of the just, set free!
Blest be thy memory, and blest
  Thy bright example be!

Faith, perseverance, zeal,
  Language of light and power,
Love,—prompt to act and quick to feel,—
  Marked thee, till life's last hour.

Now,—toil and conflict o'er,—
  Go, take with saints thy place;
But go, as each hath gone before,
  A sinner saved by grace.

Lord Jesus! to thy hands
  Our Pastor we resign;
And now we wait thine own commands;—
  We were not his, but thine.

* Hymn 54 in the *Church Psalmist.*

Thou art thy Church's head;
  And when the members die,
Thou raisest others in their stead;—
  To thee we lift our eye.

On thee our hopes depend;
  We gather round our Rock;
Send whom thou wilt, but condescend
  Thyself to feed thy flock.

He also read appropriate selections of Scripture. Rev. EDWARD TAYLOR, (Congregational,) followed in a singularly beautiful and touching prayer, which melted all hearts, and closed amid the tears and sobs of the vast audience. The choir then sang:

DEATH OF THE RIGHTEOUS.*

How blest the righteous when he dies,—
  When sinks a weary soul to rest!
How mildly beam the closing eyes!
  How gently heaves the expiring breast!

So fades a summer-cloud away;
  So sinks the gale when storms are o'er;
So gently shuts the eye of day;
  So dies a wave along the shore.

A holy quiet reigns around,—
  A calm which life nor death destroys;
Nothing disturbs that peace profound,
  Which his unfettered soul enjoys.

---

* Hymn 624 in the *Church Psalmist.*

Farewell, conflicting hopes and fears!
  Where lights and shades alternate dwell;
How bright th' unchanging morn appears!
  Farewell, inconstant world, farewell!

Life's duty done, as sinks the day,
  Light from its load the spirit flies;
While heaven and earth combine to say,—
  "How blest the righteous when he dies!"

Then, with a voice modulated to the tones of sorrow, though at times rising in eloquent strains of eulogy, Rev. SAMUEL HASKELL, (Baptist,) delivered the Funeral Discourse.*

At the close of the discourse, which was listened to throughout with tearful solemnity and the deepest interest, Rev. J. D. HEMENWAY, (Methodist,) offered a brief prayer, and the choir tenderly and beautifully sang:

"THERE IS SWEET REST IN HEAVEN."†

Though often here we're weary,
  There is sweet rest above,
A rest that is eternal,
  Where all is peace and love;
O let us then press forward,
  That glorious rest to gain:
We'll soon be free from sorrow,
  From toil, and care, and pain.
    There is sweet rest, &c.

---

* Published in a subsequent part of this volume.

† Page 360 of the *Eclectic Tune Book.* This hymn was an especial favorite with the deceased.

Loved ones have gone before us,
  They beckon us away,
O'er aërial plains they're soaring,
  Blest in eternal day;
But we are in the army,
  And dare not leave our post;
We'll fight until we conquer
  The foe's most mighty host.
    There is sweet rest, &c.

Our Saviour will be with us,
  E'en to our journey's end,
In every sore affliction,
  His present help to lend.
He never will grow weary,
  Though often we request;
He'll give us grace to conquer,
  And take us home to rest.
    There is sweet rest, &c.

All glory to the Father,
  Who gives us every good;
All glory be to Jesus,
  Who bought us with his blood;
And glory to the Spirit,
  Who keeps us to the end;
To the Triune God be glory,
  The sinner's only friend.
    There is sweet rest, &c.

The benediction was pronounced by Rev. Mr. HEMENWAY; and the form of the beloved Pastor was borne from its accustomed place, never to return. A procession, in carriages and on foot—*all mourners*—extending in length a half mile or more, moved with it to the cemetery, where a hymn was sung, chiefly by his ministerial brethren:

DEATH AND BURIAL OF SAINTS.*

Unveil thy bosom, faithful tomb!
  Take this new treasure to thy trust,
And give these sacred relics room
  To seek a slumber in the dust.

Nor pain, nor grief, nor anxious fear,
  Invade thy bounds;—no mortal woes
Can reach the peaceful sleeper here,
  While angels watch the soft repose.

So Jesus slept; God's dying Son,
  Passed through the grave, and blessed the bed;
Rest here, blest saint!—till, from his throne,
  The morning break, and pierce the shade.

Break from his throne, illustrious morn!
  Attend, O earth! his sovereign word;
Restore thy trust:—a glorious form
  Shall then arise to meet the Lord.

Prayer was offered at the head of the grave, and benediction given by Rev. Mr. Bryant, of Niles. The corpse was then lowered to its final resting-place, on a lovely eminence in the "Mountain Home," and the sad procession turned homeward.

---

* Hymn 618 in the *Church Psalmist.*

MEMORIAL MEETING.

THE MEMORIAL MEETING.

In the evening of the day on which the funeral services were solemnized, a meeting was held in the Presbyterian Church, in Kalamazoo, principally to give the ministers from abroad an opportunity to express publicly their sense of the great loss sustained by themselves and the Church, and to present their recollections of their deceased co-laborer. The meeting was numerously attended by a deeply interested congregation.

Addresses were made during the evening by Rev. Messrs. Hoyt, Bryant, Bradley, Chapin, McCorkle, and Gaston; and Hon. E. C. Walker, of Detroit, responded briefly to an invitation to speak. All the addresses breathed the spirit of the warmest fraternal affection for the departed Pastor, and expressed a profound grief for the personal and public loss experienced in his death. Many interesting reminiscences of personal intercourse, and incidents of his ministerial and social life, were also given. Near the close of the meeting, Rev. E. Taylor, of Kalamazoo, rose and said there were hundreds who sympathized in these utterances of sorrow, but who had no means of public expression for their feelings. As the voice of this large class, he would read a beautiful tribute to the memory of the deceased, which had been placed upon the threshold of his study that morning, by some person to him unknown:

Died, March 23d, Rev. WM. S. HUGGINS, *Pastor of the Presbyterian Church, Kalamazoo.*

The Master calleth—
And the hands which labored patiently
Are folded, pulseless, over the still heart
Which loved so well. Dead on the field,
With all the scars in front, his harness on,
The battle-cry still sounding—"On for God,
And for the love of Jesus!"
So fell our brother, leader of a host
Whose warfare angels watched with eager hope,
As kindly bending from their own bright home,
Or passing swiftly as they minister
To those who faint with toil.

The Master calleth—
And the dear voice which led the host
From earth up to th' eternal throne,
On wings of faith, in prayer, is hushed;
The eye, that open window of the soul,
Beaming so bright with love and joy, is closed;
While all the sweet associations,

Love's interchanges and life's hopes,
Are numbered with the things that were.
Rest, soldier, rest. Thy sun went down at noon,
But, as thy girded armor witnesseth,
Thou wert ever ready for the call;
And the warm tears which fall like rain
Above thee, like pearls are set within the crown
Thy glorious Master has laid up for those
Who, like the Gentile Teacher, fought the fight,
And kept the faith unswerving.
Rest, soldier, rest—thy Master called for thee.

W. G. B.

Rev. O. P. Hoyt, of Elkhart, Ind., added a few fitting remarks, and presented, as the expression of "ministers from the different parts of the State, and of various denominations," the following

RESOLUTIONS.

Resolved, 1. That we heartily thank our brother Haskell for his truthful, genial, and appreciative sketch of the life, character, and labors of our dear, departed brother, whom we have this day followed to his quiet home.

Resolved, 2. That it is to us a pleasure and a privilege to add our most unqualified concurrence with that faithful delineation; and we solicit a copy for preservation in some permanent and printed form, as a memorial of one whom none knew but to love.

Resolved, 3. That, inadequate as any expression of sympathy must be to alleviate the sorrows occasioned by this great bereavement, we do, nevertheless, in all the fullness of our stricken hearts, tender our condolence to the bereaved family of our beloved brother, and also to the people of his congregation, in the faith and hope that this great sorrow may, "through the prayers of many," become the occasion of great spiritual and eternal consolation.

The resolutions were unanimously adopted, and the Memorial Meeting closed with prayer by Rev. E. DAVIES, of Battle Creek.

FUNERAL DISCOURSE.

FUNERAL DISCOURSE.

The pastors of the several Churches in Kalamazoo have for years enjoyed with each other most intimate fraternal associations. Each week we have met together to join our prayers, to commune of our Christian and official experiences, to talk of the doctrines preached unto the people, and to counsel over the interests of religion and morals in our field. And in other ways much endearing social intercourse has been enjoyed between us.

Together we have planned and conducted many Union meetings in these sanctuaries and places of prayer—never one like the present! This week is all new to us. Its earliest dawn found us all hastening through the breaking darkness to the house of one of our number for whom the messenger of death had come. We were to go up with him towards the gate of Paradise, that Sabbath morning opening for his admission. He was already departing. We accompanied him with many friends, to that boundary where mortal feet must stop, and the spirit alone advance into the presence of the King, and there we parted hands—not hearts—with Brother HUGGINS.

It is these close and tender associations that have led friends to feel that our broken circle may fitly be called to lead the funeral services for him who is taken from us. Most of the feelings of our hearts would rather have selected our seats with the mourners. Brother Ministers of his own denomination, who are here from different homes, whom he strongly loved, and to whom the leading part to-day would ordinarily have fallen, we are sure we shall have your sympathy in our service of saddened love.

William Sidney Huggins was born in New Haven, Conn., March 19th, 1822, and consequently passed out of his fortieth year on his sick bed a week ago to-day. At two years of age he was left, with two little brothers, fatherless; as his own little ones are to-day. But he was not a child to take advantage of the absence of paternal restraint. He was loving and dutiful to his widowed mother, and soon grew to be her sympathizing helper. It is not in the recollection of his mother that he ever needed correction. Toward his brothers he was ever kind and affectionate, never having with them a quarrel, and never willing to be out of their society. When in later years one of them was taken away by death, it planted a sorrow in his heart which remained tenderly sensitive through his whole life. As a boy of the city he shrunk from all vicious street associations. His evenings he always chose to spend at home, reading aloud to his mother, or otherwise gladdening the little domestic circle; unless, indeed, he went in that circle to religious or other profitable assemblages. So that the counsels to boys and young men, as to their companionships and manner of spending evenings, which many of you have so often heard, and I think heard in his last utterances from this pulpit, are enforced by the happy experiences of his own boyhood and young manhood, and are embalmed now with your remembrances of his personal character as a youth. Repeatedly have I heard him express wonder and pain that boys are not seen with their parents more generally in our prayer and conference rooms, and cite his own different early habits, with their beneficial effects.

At sixteen he entered Yale College, and graduated at twenty, with the class of 1842. Like so many other students, his conversion to Christ dates from his college course, when the element of godliness was planted in his nature, to transform the naturally amiable into the graciously holy young man. This change was professed by uniting with the Congregational Church in the College.

He himself gives, in a sketch furnished to the Secretary of his Class, according to their custom, the following record of the way over which Providence has led him since his graduation:

"Spent three years as Private Tutor in the family of James Hamilton Couper, Esq., Glynn Co., Ga., and then three years as student in the Theological Department of Yale College, though absent during the last half of 1846 on a voyage to Europe for the benefit of his health. He was licensed to preach in the summer of 1847, and after leaving the Seminary in 1848, preached for some months in Hatfield, Mass.; but the failure of his eyes obliged him to decline settling there and to give up close application to study for nearly two years. During this time he spent a summer (1849) in Andover, Mass., and preached nearly a year in Brunswick Co., Va. In the years 1851 and 1852 he preached in various places: Natick, Mass., Reading, Pa., East

Medway and Framingham, Mass., and for several months in Beloit, Wis. At length, Nov. 9th, 1852, he was ordained Pastor of the Congregational Church in Whitewater, Wis. Early in 1853 an attack of pleurisy compelled him to give up his charge and for some time he remained unsettled. Sept. 26th, 1854, he was installed Pastor of the Presbyterian Church in Kalamazoo, Mich."

He was married in October, 1854, to Miss MARY FRANCES SMITH, daughter of Hon. Judge A. D. Smith, of Milwaukee.

His wife and four little children are left to mourn for one of the happiest and wisest of husbands and fathers. While his still widowed mother, with but one surviving son, and with the weight of three score years and ten, bows to receive this unexpected load of sorrow, still feeling that for such a son "passed into the skies," she has vastly more reason to be thankful than to be mournful.

The rest you know. "How through infirmity of the flesh he preached the Gospel unto you" until two weeks ago, when he was seized with a violent attack of Typhoid Pneumonia, which drew him so rapidly towards the grave, that he was at its mouth before we were aware. Not sooner, however, than he was prepared, nor more swiftly than he was willing. When I said to him last Saturday, "Can you leave yourself in the hands of God and say, 'It is the Lord, let him do as seemeth him good!'" his ready reply was, "Yes—— but I wish it were the end; and no more pain and suffering." He could say but little; spoke of the difficulty of rising above his physical sufferings, which now oppressed and had always followed him; reminded us of his love for us all; wished the family gathered and prayer offered, and thankfully gave me his fevered parting hand. When, the next morning, we were all summoned to his dying room, he requested several times our brief prayers, suppressed his short and moaning breathings to listen to quoted Scriptures and lines of loved hymns, and chimed his feeble voice to "Rock of Ages," and other dying-room melodies which we tried to sing. He said, "It is pleasant to go down into the valley and go up" on the other side; recognized and turned his lips to kiss mother, wife, and each of the children; responded even playfully to the prattle of the infant, and said, "comfort the babies." Being reminded of the Sabbath morning, and asked if he had anything to say for his people about to assemble, he said, "he had a great deal to say," but was satisfied with the thought that he had said all to them while in health. He struggled, however, to articulate such messages as, "Tell them to be active and zealous Christians;" "to throw away the world out of their thoughts, and the Lord will direct their minds in all things;" and requested Brother Willard, who was to supply the pulpit, to "call after service." He then sunk into apparent unconsciousness, and while we worshipped in our sanctuaries, he lay in silent and quiet breathings. Precisely at noon he died; noon of the Lord's Day, March 23d, 1862. At the noon too of a bright and holy Christian career, and a wide ministerial usefulness; his earthly services ending just as the Sabbath morning services in the sanctuaries where he was so familiar, came to their end. With the benedictions of the many thousands of Israel, his spirit rose to serve in the Temple of which the Lamb is the light.

This event, so joyous to him and so grateful to his friends in its Christian aspects, will yet cause a chastened but deep sorrow in many throughout our State, while it leaves in special bereavement the whole community in which he lived. At his responsible post, he has gradually grown in the respect, esteem and love of his people, and of an ever widening circle of friends.

His nature was most genial, and of the

highest moral tone. His abilities were good and most evenly balanced; presided over by a judgment almost intuitively right and ready in its decisions, and guided by an exceedingly fine and true sense of what is appropriate to times and circumstances. His acquisitions were extensive, and grew steadily more so to the last, under a wisely systematized and unyielding studiousness, and a diligent practical use of his knowledge—habits which, though sorely tested by constitutional ill-health, by frequent severe bodily sufferings and consequent mental depressions, and by many and varied interruptions, were yet maintained with rare regularity and success, up to and past the assault of his final sickness.

Extensive travel in this and other lands, and temporary residences in the different sections of our country, had liberalized his feelings and given a cultivated ease to his manners, but never blunted the edge of his sharp moral discernments and sensibilities, nor relaxed the stern precision of his principles and conscientious habits, nor displaced his lovely modesty, that ever shrunk from any ostentatious display of his traveled and scholarly distinctions.

His piety was that of the whole heart, developing itself in the whole life. It was not a mere sensibility, but gracious principle inwrought with his whole being. It was not natural goodness acting in religious forms. Though of this few possess more, of it few make so little account in estimating Christian character. He held himself bound to find gracious experiences in his daily inner life, and often called himself to account, and made humbling confessions to God and with his Christian companions, that these experiences were so indistinct and feeble. And before his abased self he loved to bring the exalted Saviour, and say with trustful fondness,

"Simply to Thy Cross I cling."

His piety was uniformly and eminently active. No man amongst us had a livelier or more tireless sympathy with every form of going about and doing good; and none has had feet more willing and wonted in treading these daily rounds of beneficence. Alas, that their coming will be waited for in vain henceforth: by the children of sorrow, of poverty, and of awakened religious interest; by the stranger in our gates, the young men in our streets, and shops, and stores, and homes; by the aged and the children, the wanderers from Christ's fold, and the lost in the dark world.

Nor was he satisfied with a personal activity in himself. The burden of the Lord upon him was that all Christians should be workers in the vineyard. For this he prayed, and conversed, and planned, and plead; elaborating schemes of beneficence for individuals and for the Church and Society, through which the seed could be sown beside all waters, from those by our own doors to those in the far deserts of heathenism.

As a preacher he was Scriptural, appropriate, practical, and earnest. His aim was the conversion of the impenitent, and the holiness of the regenerate. Simply to entertain an audience through an appointed service was in his view a prostitution of the momentous work with which the preacher is charged of God. Merely to render a people intelligent in Bible and Christian knowledge, though he labored in this so hard and well, he conceived of as but a means to the preacher's end, not the end itself. It was the heart and the life that he was after, not the pleased crowd, at ease in their sins, whatever of worldly advantages they might proffer. It was heart and hand knowledge that he sought to impart, not mere head knowledge. Hence he was faithful. If he ever misjudged as to what ought to be preached, he never hesitated to preach what he thought ought to be preached. And to this he added the higher and rarer faithfulness of speaking the truth in love; with every just consideration for the feelings of those whom the truth might condemn, coupled with fidelity to their souls, and to the cause of God. So that nothing but misapprehension or perversity itself could take offense.

In short, our calmest judgment could ever join with our warm affection and say to him, what we believe our Master would apply, "Beloved, thou doest faithfully whatsoever thou doest."

I have not drawn this sketch from fancy, but with the living original continually before me, and compelling myself to use only truthful colors. I am glad to find it resembling one shown me this morning from the hand of an older friend, and one in some relations more intimate—his class and room-mate in College, Hon. E. C.

WALKER, Esq., of Detroit. You will be grateful for the following passages which I read from his letter:

"He entered Yale College in 1838, and graduated in a class numbering a hundred and five, in 1842. He was a contemporary in College with Donald G. Mitchell, ('Ike Marvel,') Richard Storrs Willis, and Rev. A. Eldridge, of Detroit; and a class-mate of Profs. Hadley and J. A. Porter, now of Yale College, and Gen'l Runyon, of New Jersey, and Rev. A. H. Clapp, of Providence. He graduated with high honors. He was a universal favorite in his class. His scholarship was not, like that of many, in some special department; but his intellect was roundly and fully developed, and every department of science and literature received his attention, and aided to make the thorough student. I think his most distinguishing characteristic in College was his elegant and graceful style of composition, which was always, to my mind, his charming characteristic as a preacher.

* * "In Georgia he formed many friendships which ended only with his life. His summers were spent at the plantation on St. Simond's Island, and the rest of the year upon the upland. His letters to me during this period are full of pleasant sketches

of his every day life. Having the ministry in view, he entered at once into his Master's service, and devoted himself to the good of the colored population about him; with the aid and sympathy of Judge Couper, whom he always described as a thoroughly educated and polished gentleman and scholar. He saw slavery in its happiest lights, yet came home with a quiet but decided opinion that it was the curse of the white man of the South; and in the late struggles of our country this experience of his youth only deepened and made clear the currents of his patriotism.

* * "His southern residence seemed to have undermined his constitution, and ever since his health has been precarious, never robust.

* * "He was a thoroughly earnest, sincere man and Christian. He labored for souls, and not as a hireling for outward prosperity and the mere triumphs of success. In his last letter to me, dated March 6th, 1862, he yearned over his people, as a father over his first born son. 'Oh Lord, revive thy work,' was on his pen and in his heart. His merits as a pastor, to us who looked at him from without his congregation, were those of a practical kind, that succeeded in accomplishing results, in moulding his church and building it up in every good word and work. His church had become one of the most systematically liberal and benevolent

churches in the State. His pulpit powers were of a high order, and had God spared his health and life, there was no church in the land that might not be proud of such a pastor and such a preacher. His social and domestic virtues you doubtless appreciate and admire. My house was his home in Detroit, and his agreeable manners and gentlemanly deportment to all, won the respect of all who met him. He is a loss to the ministry in Michigan, which, I fear, will not soon be supplied.

"He was a Presbyterian from conviction and from choice, but was no sectarian, and was always ready to give the right hand of fellowship to any man or body of men who approached him in the name and with the spirit of Christ." * * *

Such being the man whom God has permitted you for nearly eight years to possess as your Pastor, afflicted people of his charge, what account think you will He require as to your improvement of the precious gift? While we all as a community are debtors, how great is the claim which has run up in your account!

If you will allow of a text at the end

of my address, I have one which I wish to print in your hearts beside the likeness of this dear servant which you are henceforth to bear there—a text which, I happen to know, was well understood by your Pastor, and employed to bring to him sympathy from an Apostle in glory, in times when earthly sympathies were insufficient.

This text occurs in the second chapter of the Epistle to the Philippians; where the Apostle Paul most affectionately urges those for whom he was laboring to so live that he might rejoice in the Day of Christ that he had not run in vain, neither labored in vain, and then at the close of his exhortations breaks forth in these strong words:

"YEA, AND IF I BE OFFERED UPON THE SACRIFICE AND SERVICE OF YOUR FAITH, I JOY AND REJOICE WITH YOU ALL."

In what would Paul joy and rejoice? It is told us in his Jewish way, and needs simply this exposition: When, in the ancient Sanctuary service, the victim for a burnt offering had been prepared, the carefully dressed parts of the animal being laid upon the altar, and the fire beneath them enkindled, then the Priest stood beside the offering, and poured upon it a libation, of choicest wine and purest oil, mingled with fine flour, whence a rich fragrance, emitted by the burning flame, went up as a symbol of Jehovah's pleased acceptance of the sacrifice. Now the sacrifice which the Apostle sought to offer before God was that of a holy, practical faith in the people of his care: a faith that should not be a creed of the head, but a state and habit of the soul; turning it trustingly and lovingly Godward, purifying from all sin through the blood of Christ, warming with steady life all holy activities, and shining strongly in the world with the lighted truths of all Scripture. Such worth, in Paul's account, had this gracious faith, as constituting its possessor a receiver and disburser of all spiritual and useful gifts, that he would gladly sacrifice his life, if necessary, in helping men to attain and perfect it in their inner and outer lives. Striving to present it as an offering to God, he would joyfully be not only the ministering priest, but the consuming libation also; pouring out his life in labors, or privations, or martyrdom, that believers might be multiplied and made holy in character and useful in the world. This Paul was willing to do, and this it fell to him to do.

Need I say that WILLIAM S. HUGGINS came into closer sympathy with Paul, as here seen, than most ministers come? God's providence brought him there, as it brought Paul there. In counting the cost of his service for you, his people, he *had* to include his life itself. His state of health made it impossible for him to serve you well without, more literally than any other man I have known, pouring out his life in the service, *from week to week*. Every Sabbath night found the fountains of his vitality drained almost to the bottom. Then two nights and days of prostration, with the aching head and the deathly sickness, yet not in idleness, and, the vital reservoirs beginning to fill again, he returned to stay by the altar of service and pour there anew the costly libation.

And though this was the cost, did he not serve you well? Did he slight his work, in the pulpit or the parish? Did he, even as frequently as he ought, relieve himself of its burden for a week or a day, or a single service, so fearful was he that it might suffer from his absence or his enjoyment of relief in the pulpit?

And did he not rejoice in his service, notwithstanding it was thus constantly draining off his life? Did any one ever hear him complain of the hardships of the ministry, or covet the easier allotments in life? "I will very gladly spend and be spent for you," was language which his fear of boasting may never have allowed you to hear him appropriate to himself, but which, in the home-ear of his nearest earthly friend, was often spoken.

Yes, let me tell you how this labored yet joyful sacrifice of his life for your salvation and Christian usefulness had so become the habit of his being, that it was the most prominent feature in his dying scene. When his thoughts were left to himself, they seemed constantly laboring at the wonted tasks and cares of his ministry. "I am in perplexity"—"There are two points"—"I can go no further"—"I am sick"—"Who will preach next Sabbath?" In such fragments of sentences, the whole of which he could not articulate, we were affected in seeing how in imagination he was toiling on in the study, the pulpit, and the solicitudes of a faithful pastor: draining off the last drops of life upon "the sacrifice and service of your faith."

And where has he not shown the same spirit? How he knit his whole life to your whole life, and spent himself in struggles to rise and bear you up to the higher Christian life! Your social life and home life, your business life and civil life, your public interests of common and higher education, and all true reform and advancement in society,—he has woven himself with it all, and plied his strength unsparingly for its elevation. Into how many places he had thus wrought himself we but partly know as yet. We shall learn as we find the vacancies whence he is now withdrawn. It will be long before we find the last of them, or fill the first.

Ah, my afflicted friends, if from such a libation, poured upon the altar of your spiritual welfare, there do not arise sweetly to God a savor of life, what a savor of *death* there must go up! O that this precious outpoured life might now kindle upon you from the fire of the Holy Ghost, in flames of a new and holy devotement!

I have wished for a moment that your dear Pastor could have lived to see the one more ingathering towards which the tokens among you have been pointing, and his soul so eagerly pressing. That the enlarged and more solemnly attentive audiences might, as a harvest of souls, have ripened and been garnered under his eye, and we have seen his joy, as we have seen it in the harvests of the past. But the Lord of the field and the laborers knows best, and has not made our brother a loser by calling him to the Father's House.

Nor is it too late for you yet to minister that joy to him in Heaven, which he was not permitted to see on earth. Some of us—who first the Master knoweth—shall soon go up and rejoin our departed friend. Would it not be pleasant, for the one thus next honored, to be a bearer of despatches to him that many whom he had sought as lost, are found? That many dead, over whom he wept, are alive; and that the people of God, for whose holy living he struggled to the last, are all "zealous and active" amid the sheaves?

The joy of Paul in Heaven is not yet at the highest degree of the scale, though filling all his capacities as it ascends. "The day of Christ" has yet to reveal to him how far he has not "run in vain, neither labored in vain," and thus raise his rejoicings to far warmer heights.

And so, thank God, the beloved servant, whose form rests sweetly here, where it has so often trembled in weariness and sickness, and whose spirit is now completely blessed, may yet, from new arrivals in Paradise, and from the great all-revealing Day, have his joy raised higher and higher through the faithfulness of you who are in Christ, and the salvation of you who are out of Christ. O may it be his, with Christ and through Christ, to see of the travail of Christ's soul, of which he has been here a partaker, and be satisfied, as an humble partaker in Christ's eternal satisfaction!

With these words, and especially the words of the text to which I have cited you, pressed strongly upon your hearts, as the interpreter to you of your Pastor's life, and the preacher to you from his grave, I count my present duty done.

The mourning have many to sympathize with and counsel them, some of whom may more fitly than myself assume that office. And the less public will be the more suitable occasions for our utterances to them: so heavily afflicted, yet already, and we trust ever to be, so abundantly sustained and peacefully comforted. May God bless in this bereavement the family and bosom friends, the Church, the ministry, and our stricken community!

Three Sermons to Young Men.

I.

THE BIBLE THE YOUNG MAN'S HAND-BOOK.

PREACHED SABBATH EVENING, FEB. 2, 1862.*

PSALM CXIX: 9.

"WHEREWITHAL SHALL A YOUNG MAN CLEANSE HIS WAY? BY TAKING HEED THERETO, ACCORDING TO THY WORD."

WHEN the traveler is leaving London for the Continent, he makes up his mind whither he will go, and seeks for information as to the best routes and the most desirable modes of traveling. He soon finds that hand-books have been prepared, each with special reference to some one or more of the countries which he pro-

* Published in pamphlet form soon after, by request of a number of young men of the congregation.

poses to visit. He provides himself with these, glad to get such reliable guides, and not to be dependent upon the uncertain information which he might seek or find upon the way.

But when it is simply "the way of life" along which the traveler is journeying, he generally either asks no questions, or asks only such as pertain to matters of subordinate importance. He neglects to inquire what kind of road it is he has set out upon, what direction it takes, to what liabilities it is subject, and toward what particular point it tends.

Fortunately, these questions are asked for him, and the same kind Providence which has asked them, has answered them. They are summed up in the words of the text: "Wherewithal shall a young man cleanse his way? By taking heed thereto, according to thy Word." The question is asked with special reference to youth, because it needs to be asked and answered in advance of manhood and age, and because, if the answer is not heard and heeded during youth, in a majority of cases it might as well never have been answered.

In accordance with the question and answer of the text, let me to-night commend to you, especially to such of you as are young, the Bible as the "Hand-book" of "this way of life." I say *commend* it, for I could not *force* it upon you if I would. It is your prerogative to accept or reject whatever counsel may be given to you; to believe or disbelieve whatever guide-boards you may read, and whatever words you may hear, as you pursue this way; to trust to the whims and impressions and impulses of each passing day, or to make the Bible from this time forth the Hand-book for your journey. This is your prerogative, and no one would take it away from you. Yet at the same time it is the privilege of those of us who believe in the Bible, and believe in it as a book to be followed as well as possessed, to ask you candidly to weigh its claims in the light of certain facts which concern you and all of us.

Let me to-night call your attention to three such facts.

I. And first, let me remind you that God made you for a definite end, and that end was His own glory and your highest good.

In Paul's Epistle to the Romans we read: "For of him, and through him, and to him are all things, to whom be glory forever." In the book of Proverbs we read that "the Lord hath made all things for himself." So also in the Epistle to Colossians: "All things were created by him and for him." And in the first of Peter: "That God in all things may be glorified through Jesus Christ."

Paul's exhortation to the Corinthians

points us to the great end of our being: "Whether ye eat or drink, or whatsoever ye do, do all to the glory of God."

There is danger, however, especially with the young, that this language will be misunderstood; that the "glory of God" will be little more than an abstract idea, true enough, perhaps, as a theoretical end of living, and an end for theologians to talk about, but not a practical end, within the familiar range of one's every-day vision. Hence our Catechism has very happily added a phrase, in defining what "man's chief end" is; it is "to glorify God, and to enjoy him forever." This brings out the important truth that we have a partnership with God in the end for which we were made. We were not only made for his glory, but for our own enjoyment; and his glory includes and comprehends our highest enjoyment, if we will only have it so. And there is another interesting truth included here, which may be a little more fully expressed. It is this, that the "chief end" for which man was made was not only that he should enjoy God forever, but that God should enjoy him forever. It was for mutual enjoyment.

When "God saw every thing that He had made, and behold, it was very good," is it not meant that there was in it all a good for Him, as well as for birds and beasts, and the human pair, and for angels; and especially that a gratification and a glory were to be derived from those whom He had created in his own image?

God's glory, then, for which we are to live and labor, is not an abstract idea, a cold logical or theological conclusion, like the conclusion of a mathematical demonstration. God's blessedness is included in His glory, and our happiness also. When reminded, therefore, that God made you for a definite end, do not fail to see that this purposed end was a mutual good, and a mutual glory.

How desirable, now, that this purposed end should be fulfilled in the case of every one of you! God desires it. The angels would say that you ought to desire it. And God not only desires it, but from the beginning He has been doing all he consistently could to secure it. The most important of the instrumentalities which He is employing for this purpose is the Bible.

More than fifteen hundred years in process of preparation; the product, under the guidance of the Spirit, of more than thirty different writers, and made up, in beautiful combination and wonderful harmony, of history and poetry and prophecy, of biographies and parables, of precepts and promises, of descriptions of this world and of the world to come, *its one, great, comprehensive aim* is to teach you the chief end for which God made you, and to teach you how to fulfill that end.

See, now, how miserably man, without

the Bible, misses this end. Look at the South Sea Islander, and the Bushmen of South Africa! Read the first chapter of Paul's Epistle to the Romans, and remember that that fearful description of those who know not God, and glorify Him not as God, applies not only with striking accuracy, as all missionaries testify, to those whom we commonly call the heathen, but to the most enlightened pagan nations—to all among whom the light of the Bible does not shine. Individuals may be discovered here and there, who stand somewhat above the common level of idolatry and ignorance and degradation; but they, if they raise the question as to the chief end of man, grope in the dark in their search to find it.

But we need not go to the ends of the earth, or to the far-off nations of cultivated paganism. See how miserably man misses this end, even amid all the restraining influences of a Christian civilization, when he throws away his Bible and casts off all fear of God. In every Christian community of any considerable numbers, there are multitudes of men whose motives and whose end in life are not one whit higher than those of the heathen. What is their goal—I do not say their goal of life, for they do not give dignity to their career by any forethought of a lifetime—but what is the goal of each day's little round? The lowest forms of sensual indulgence, amid the most disgusting associations. The end for which they live is no higher than that of the brute, and in stooping to such an end, a man degrades himself below the brute.

O man, how hast thou fallen, and on how low a level thou every day dost walk, and to what low depths dost stoop, in worse than "beastly drink," in vulgar and obscene and heaven-defying talk, and in practices most foul and full of outrage upon the very name of man!

But there are multitudes besides, who would shrink from the thought of being identified with this low and lustful and almost hopeless class, and whom, as yet, thanks to the gracious influences around them, we are not obliged to classify with these, who are nevertheless identified with them to this extent, that they are in the same broad road, and that they are missing life's great end. And he who simply misses the one path that leads to the mountain's summit, where shelter and rest await the traveler; he who simply misses the one path when the storm is gathering and the night is coming on, what will his end be, no matter whether the last you saw of him was only a little way off the road, or half-way down some steep declivity?

To lose sight of life's great end is to lose the way to happiness and heaven. The man at the wheel might as well neglect to look at the compass, and undertake to steer by the bowsprit. And yet it is to just this that our nature is extremely liable—to neglect to determine upon any life-long course, to leave the chart unrolled in the chest, to steer by the desire that is uppermost and that "heads" us, whether this way or that; to use eye and ear and tongue and hand and foot, mind and body, without end and aim; sight-seeing, novel-reading, card-playing, news-gathering, tattling, dancing, handling toys and busy with trifles, instead of handling the implements of life's work, and wielding the weapons of life's warfare for glory and for good.

What multitudes there are—and oh how easily the young are recruited to fill their ranks!—what multitudes who seem to live only to laugh and talk, to walk and ride, to escape being alone and to go into company, to repeat jokes and scandal, to see showy trifles and to hear and tell some new thing, or from day to day repeat the same stale things, to eat and drink and dress, though not perhaps to sleep, until night is turned into day, and mind and body are wearied with unnatural use. Not that all the items of this catalogue are wholly wrong in themselves; but to live only for this—how wide of the mark which Heaven has set before each deathless soul!

I heard it said the other day, that it was the recent remark of a gentleman, whose opportunities for judging had not been limited, that "there are not half a dozen young men in this community who are living with any end in view!" I do not say that I believe this. On the contrary, I should say at once that the statement was an exaggerated one, though I do not know how great or how little the exaggeration was; but I repeat the remark as justifying me, if justification be needed, in thus urging the point upon you, that God made you for a definite end. I repeat it, because it is sometimes well that we should know what others say of us; because it may be well that the young men in our shops and stores and offices, in our homes and upon our streets, should know what judgment business men are forming of them. If it is a slander, you need not fear it, and there may be a salutary warning in it; and if it is not a slander, it may set you to thinking, and sober thought and the Word of God may bring before you life's great end, and the result may be repentance and reformation, God's glory and your present and eternal good.

Liable thus, as you especially are who are surrounded by the attractions and subject to the impulses of youth, to forget, to lose sight of, to miss the great end of life, let me urge you to take heed to your way—to its direction, and to the end toward which it is tending—according to God's Word. Let me urge you to make the Bible the guide of your youth; the counsels of the Bible, rather than the example and the tempting suggestions or taunts of your companions; the teachings of this Word of God, I must add with pain, rather than the example of some who profess to be the people of God!

II. Let me remind you, secondly, not only that you are made for a definite and high end, which you are so liable to forget or lose sight of, but that with this end distinctly in view, left to your unaided self, you will never seriously pursue it; that resolve, and even strive as you may, to do so, you will find that you are at war with yourself, or you will be at war with yourself, whether you find it out or not; that your own nature will hinder and successfully oppose all your attempts at true progress and real elevation; that a secret foe in your own breast will deceive you and turn you aside, or turn you back to your eternal ruin; *and that with this fact and the philosophy of it,* the Bible, and the Bible alone, acquaints you; that against this secret foe the Bible, and the Bible alone, will faithfully warn you and arm you, and successfully aid you and give you the victory.

Perhaps I cannot more successfully tell you just what I mean than by quoting a passage from a popular English author, who writes especially for boys and young men, and has had the credit of speaking to them in a true and wise and manly way. I the more readily avail myself of his language, because it did not originate with the pulpit. It is not simply professional, as you might regard the utterances of the minister. It is not a formal exposition of Scripture doctrine, against which you might be prejudiced. It is an earnest man's setting forth of a fact which he discovers in himself, and which, as a philosophic observer, he comes in contact with, out in the world, as he studies men.*

Two young men stand fronting one another, "the younger," who in his heart is secretly meditating, though half unconsciously, a great wrong toward which his passions are strongly drifting him—a wrong which his older companion, acting the part of a true friend, has just honestly but somewhat bluntly rebuked—"the younger, writhing with a sense of shame and outraged pride, and longing for a fierce answer" to language he has just uttered—"a fierce answer, or a blow, anything to give vent to the furies which were tearing him."

They soon part, and the younger is striding up and down by himself in the pale moonlight.

"Poor fellow! it was no pleasant walking ground for him. Shall we follow him up and down in his tramp? We have most of us walked the like

---

* Tom Brown at Oxford, Vol. I., 252.

marches, I suppose, at one time or another in our lives. The memory of them is by no means one which we can dwell on with pleasure. Times they were of blinding and driving storm and howling winds, out of which voices, as of evil spirits, spoke close in our ears—tauntingly, temptingly, whispering to the mischievous wild beast which lurks in the bottom of all our hearts, now, 'Rouse up! art thou a man and darest not do this thing?' now, 'Rise, kill and eat; it is thine, wilt thou not eat it? Shall the flimsy scruples of this teacher, or the sanctified cant of that, bar thy way and balk thee of thine own? Thou hast strength; brave them—brave all things in earth, or heaven, or hell; put out thy strength, and be a man!' Then did not the wild beast within us shake itself and feel its power, sweeping away all the 'Thou shalt *nots*,' which the law wrote up before us in letters of fire, with the '*I will*' of hardy, godless self-assertion? And all the while—which alone made the storm more dreadful to us—was there not the still, small voice, never to be altogether silenced by the roarings of the tempest of passion, by the evil voices, by our own violent attempts to stifle it; the still, small voice appealing to the man, the true man within us, which is made in the image of God, calling on him to assert his dominion over the wild beast—to obey, and conquer, and live? Ay! and though we may have followed the other voices, have we not, while following them, confessed in our hearts that all true strength and nobleness and manliness was to be found in the other path? Do I say that most of us have had to tread the path, and fight this battle? Surely, I might have said all of us; all at least who have passed the bright days of their boyhood. The keen and clear intellect, no less than the dull and heavy; the weak, the cold, the nervous, no less than the strong and passionate of body. The arms and the field have been diverse; can have been the same, I suppose, to no two men, but the battle must have been the same to all. One here and there may have had a foretaste of it as a boy; but it is the young man's battle, and not the boy's, thank God for it! That most hateful and fearful of all realities, call it by what name we will—self, the natural man, the old Adam—must have risen up before each of us in early manhood, if not sooner, challenging the true man within us, to which the Spirit of God is speaking, to a struggle for life or death.

"Gird yourself, then, for the fight, my young brother, and take up the pledge which was made for you when you were a helpless child. This world and all others, time and eternity, for you hang upon the issue. This enemy must be met and vanquished—not finally, for no man, while on earth, I suppose, can say that he is slain; but when once known and recognized, met and vanquished he must be, by God's help, in this and that encounter, before you can be truly called a man; before you can really enjoy any one even of this world's good things."

"Met and vanquished," he says, "by God's help,"—by God's help, if met and vanquished at all. Now, in this conflict, how does God propose to help us? By his Word and through the Holy Spirit, and in answer to our cries for help. Concerning the character of this secret foe, and the realities and possibilities of this inward warfare, the Bible is our only competent instructor and counselor and helper.

It gives us the information which we need; it puts us upon our guard; it gives us timely exhortation and encouragement; it rebukes our unconcern and lack of vigilance; it prompts the needful prayer for help; above all, it brings us to Jesus, if we will only follow where it would lead us—to Jesus, the great Captain of Salvation. He is "a stronger" than the "strong man armed" within us, and He alone can enable us to cripple and subdue him. Hence it is that the Bible is commended to us in the question and answer of the text, though under a different figure from that which I have used. Sin is viewed as a defiler rather than as an armed foe; and either view is lamentably true. Sin is a defiler. It pollutes our hearts; it defiles our character. It makes our way of life unclean. To him who sees his own heart and life under the full light of God's truth and Spirit, the sight is a loathsome one, and his way of life, if he has followed the tendencies of his nature, shocks him and disgusts him. How must it look to angels and to the all-seeing eye of perfect purity? And the question of the text is concerning "the young man."

It does not take long for sin to make

the way of life unclean. Its work is the more apparent, and it shocks us the more, as we see it in early manhood and early womanhood; for there is a native beauty and promise, and apparent innocence about the freshness of youth. Upon such a background the shadings and dark blots and foul marks of sin are painfully striking. And often how rapidly they spread, and how dark their stain, and how foul their aspect, even before bright boyhood and beautiful girlhood are fairly out from under the father's hand and the mother's eye! How often the young man has secrets which he would not have his father, which he would blush to have his sister know! How often the young woman has and cherishes secret thoughts and feelings which far from conform to the pure example and prudent counsels of her Christian mother! How often books are carefully secreted, and read with a blush, and a loose rein given to the imagination, and conduct carefully covered up! How painful it is to witness the confidence of fathers and mothers in their sons and daughters, when to observant eyes there is a worm already in the bud, and when it is only falsehood that gives to it its seeming beauty and promise! Oh how true it is that the way even of the young needs to be cleansed! And how may it be done? By taking heed to his Word. A wonderful counselor for the young is the Bible! More kind and more faithful, often, than you will find father or mother, or the best friend you may have. If every young man and woman would make the single Book of Proverbs their counselor, how many would it save from sad mistakes and bitter regrets; how many from disgrace and ruin!

III. But let me remind you, thirdly, though time warns me that it must be briefly, that you have more than yourself to contend with—this heart, this evil nature, this old Adam within us—though this should be enough to put every one on his guard; insubordination in the camp, treachery in the citadel, is bad enough; but more than this, that you are in an enemy's country, and all along your way you are surrounded by temptations and by tempters to evil.

The Apostle Peter says, "Be sober, be vigilant, because your adversary, the devil, as a roaring lion, walketh about, seeking whom he may devour." And Peter had had some experience of that of which he speaks. Jesus had once put him on his guard, saying, "Simon, Simon, Satan hath desired to have you, that he may sift you as wheat; but I have prayed for thee, that thy faith fail not." And Judas Iscariot was what he was, because Satan had "entered into him."

I know that men make a jest of this, and that this fearful name is simply made a convenience of, for rounding off a vulgar speech; but here it is, in the Bible, in the Old Testament and in the New, and on the authority of the Son of God. It is a fearful fact, and all the more fearful that we are so unmindful of it, that in the fall of man, Satan, the great adversary of truth and righteousness, the arch-deceiver and the soul's destroyer, gained a hold, temporary it is true, but a real hold upon this world; and he reigns here, with a broken sceptre indeed, but still a powerful one. And the world is full of his emissaries and servants. Whether they are consciously laboring to promote his ends, or his unconscious tools, as we will presume they generally are, their name is legion. They throng the way of life which you are treading. Some of them are just ahead of you, and many of these, probably, are objects of your admiration; and some are just behind you, and you are conscious that their eyes are fastened upon you, though you are forgetful, perhaps, of the All-seeing Eye; and they are all around you, not consciously, perhaps, nor maliciously your enemies, but nevertheless your injurers and your destroyers, if not on your guard. They may be pleasant companions, and you may think them safe; or if you suspect that they are not altogether what they ought to be, you may intend to be upon your guard, and you doubtless feel abundantly able to take care of yourself. But the young do not know one another, and they do not know themselves. How little, in many cases, the young woman knows of the character of the men with whom she trusts herself! How little young men know the character of those with whom they associate! We are easily flattered by a little attention which others may pay us. It is not always easy to avoid their approaches. To the youth it seems a great step towards manhood to be admitted into a circle of young men a little older than himself; and it may be regarded as a lack of manhood to be in anything at all behind those of his own years. He does not like to appear singular. He does not like to be laughed at. The laugh of even a silly companion often has a power before which strong resolutions and sacred promises go down like grass before the mower's scythe. The truth is, that the heart within—this nature, often so slavishly fearful, so sensitive, so vacillating, so cowardly, so vain, so proud, so obstinate, so deceitful, so blind—the heart within is in league with these tempters without, and between the two, oh how great the danger, when the young man or the young woman goes out from beneath the shelter and the restraining influences of home into the wide, wide world! Nay, how great the danger, in places like this—though places, after all, are very much alike—how great the danger, in spite of parental influences and the restraints of home; though the difficulty in part may be, that parental influence is not what it should be, and that the restraints of home are few and feeble. But under all circumstances, between appetite and passion and weakness within, and the temptations which everywhere lurk without, how great the danger! Let a young man get only so far away from home as the door of the saloon, under the lead of two or three companions, and how great his danger! Let him be invited, amid flattering surroundings, to take his first game of cards; is he not in great danger? Smile not, my hearer, at the idea of danger, because you may have played many a game, and are not yet a gambler. Could we summon witnesses here, tales might be told that would appal you. Let impure books be put into the young man's hand, and by companions who stand ready to ridicule any boyish squeamishness which he may show, and is he not in great danger? Let him be invited to take "a social glass," amid gay companions, tempted perhaps by the sex that has suffered enough from intemperance, one would suppose, to make them shrink with horror from its first approaches; and how great his danger! Let him be decoyed by older so-called friends to her house whose "feet go down to death, whose steps take hold on hell;" let the snare be suddenly sprung upon him—he thinks he is master of himself; his mother has perfect confidence in her boy; he is his sister's pride—but who will answer for his virtue? The young man is proudly conscious of his strength. He is not as others have been before him —of this he is confident. But what is a Samson, if he is but a man, and if the thing to be achieved is but a simple negative? The hero who single-handed would storm a battery, has often paled and trembled and been defeated, when all he had to do was simply to face the enemy and say "No!" Oh how weak is man, and how pitiable his condition, left to his own unaided self! God help the young man who trusts to his native strength and to his self-respect, and to his love for his father and for her who bore him, and for the sister whose heart is bound up in his success! Stronger than all these restraining cords!—oh how often has it proved!—is this cowardly fear of man, and this love of present flattery and praise, which lurk in all our breasts.

These three facts, of which I have just reminded you, my friends, these are the basis upon which I commend to you, to-night, this Book. Made for a definite and exalted end, you will certainly lose sight of it; seeking to pursue it, and striving with all your energies to attain it, you would certainly fail, because your own nature is against you, and because you are in an enemy's country, and temptations and tempters are all around you.

Under these circumstances, the Bible alone has solved the problem of man's salvation. It knows his wants, and it boldly and lovingly meets them—not with flattery, but with truth! Its solemn finger points up to God, and points in to self. Its searching eye searches the heart to its centre. It probes diseased nature, regardless of the pain it causes. It points to the one only remedy, or to the alternative, everlasting death!

If accepted, now, my hearers, its words of cheer and promise are for you. If chosen to-night, (to-morrow we cannot be sure of) and made henceforth your Counselor and Guide, it will throw around you a strong arm of support; it will interpose a shield between you and all evil; it will show you "the pillar of cloud by day" and "the pillar of fire by night;" and at your call it will summon to your side, as your Saviour and Helper and Friend—and there is not a man, and never has been of all the race, who does not need a Saviour and a Friend—it will summon to your side, both in life and death, "a stronger" than the "strong man armed" without, "a stronger" than the "strong man armed" within!

II.

THE BIBLE THE YOUNG MAN'S COUNSELOR.

PREACHED SABBATH EVENING, FEBRUARY 23, 1862, AND REPEATED, BY REQUEST, ON THE NEXT SABBATH EVENING.

JOSHUA i. 8, 7.

"THIS BOOK OF THE LAW SHALL NOT DEPART OUT OF THY MOUTH; BUT THOU SHALT MEDITATE THEREIN DAY AND NIGHT, THAT THOU MAYEST OBSERVE TO DO ACCORDING TO ALL THAT IS WRITTEN THEREIN: FOR THEN THOU SHALT MAKE THY WAY PROSPEROUS, AND THEN THOU SHALT HAVE GOOD SUCCESS. TURN NOT FROM IT TO THE RIGHT HAND OR TO THE LEFT, THAT THOU MAYEST PROSPER* WHITHERSOEVER THOU GOEST."

THESE are the words of the Lord, addressed to Joshua. In the eleventh chapter of Numbers we read: "Joshua, the

---

* Or, as we have it in the margin, that *thou mayest do wisely*.

son of Nun, the servant of Moses, *one of his young men*." Although he is not now, as addressed in the text, a young man, yet his circumstances are somewhat analogous to those in which a young man finds himself; and certainly, the words in which this book of the law is commended to Joshua as a book of counsel and command, and a sure guide to wisdom and success, these are most appropriate words to be addressed, as I address them to-night, to every young man.

Moses had just died, and Joshua finds himself bereft of the wise counsels and strong arm on which he had been accustomed to lean; just as the young man often is without the wise head and the warm heart and the strong arm of a father to lean upon. If the father is still living, the son is often far away from home, and his father cannot be his constant counselor. Responsibilities such as Joshua never knew before, now rest upon him; and just as new and fearful responsibilities rest upon the young man standing on the threshold of active life.

"The Lord spake unto Joshua, the son of Nun, Moses' minister, saying, Moses my servant is dead; now therefore arise, go over this Jordan, thou and all this people, unto the land which I do give to them. Only be thou strong and very courageous, that thou mayest observe to do according to all the law which Moses my servant commanded thee. This book of the law shall not depart out of thy mouth; but thou shalt meditate therein day and night, that thou mayest observe to do according to all that is written therein: for then thou shalt make thy way prosperous, and then thou shalt have good success. Turn not from it to the right hand or to the left, that thou mayest do wisely whithersoever thou goest."

What the Jordan was to Joshua and the children of Israel, youth is to the children of men everywhere—the dividing line beyond which lies the land of promise. And if Joshua then needed this solemn injunction and this word of encouragement, as they applied to the law of Moses, equally does the young man need them as they apply to the whole Bible. Well is it, as the young man stands upon the border of this promised land, if he feels, as Joshua felt, that it is full of foes, and that it can only be possessed as it is first subdued, and that it can be subdued only as its battles shall be fought according to the Word and in the strength of the Lord of hosts. Well is it, as he stands upon the threshold of active life, if the young man makes the Bible his counselor. Even though he be highly privileged in the counsels of his father and mother, and though he have faithful employers and kind and judicious friends to give him the benefit of their experience, and suitable admonition and encouragement, he still needs another—a more faithful, a more constant, and a wiser counselor than any of these. Such a counselor is the Bible; one which he may always have by his side—one which embodies the sympathy and the wisdom of Heaven in his behalf—and one which will always speak the right word at the right time. Without the Bible, indeed, for his chosen counselor, there is danger that he will throw all other wise counsels to the winds, and follow only the counsels of foolishness.

I. The young man needs to make the Bible his counselor, I remark, in the first place, as he stands upon the threshold of *social* life.

Social life is something more than laughing and talking, and eating and drinking, and walking and riding together. Bar-rooms and ball-rooms are not essential to it; nor are brilliantly lighted parlors and gay parties. It is not limited to the evening hours. It is not controled by fashion. We are moving amid its scenes almost every hour of the day. It includes all the relations by which the Creator has bound us together and made us dependent upon one another. It has its obligations and labors, as well as its pleasures and pastimes. It makes its demands upon our intellectual as well as our animal nature. It appeals to conscience and taste, as well as to passion and fashion. It is at once the source of the highest happiness and of the greatest misery which we can experience from any earthly source. It admits of, and it often calls for, true heroism. It is full of dangers—dangers to ourselves and to others. It is full of temptations—temptations to excess in what is in itself proper, and temptations to indulgence in what is improper and forbidden. God may be served in social life, and is to be, though the temptation is to serve mammon, and, in serving mammon, to serve Satan.

As social life, now, opens up before a young man—eager, impatient, ambitious, confiding, easily flattered, easily led, wild and wilful as the young man naturally is, to a greater or less extent—he needs a counselor, now to instruct him, now to stimulate him, now to encourage him, now to put him on his guard, now to rebuke him and solemnly warn him; a secret and constant counselor, one that shall be unseen and unheard, save by himself, even in the midst of a crowded circle, and one that shall be by when the battle is going on in the solemn silence of the heart's inmost chamber, when there is no eye to see save the Adversary's and the All-seeing eye.

He not only needs to be well-informed and faithfully admonished in regard to the dangers which beset the social side of his nature, but to be counseled in regard to his duties. Society has claims upon every man; not only his family and his place of business, but his neighborhood, those with whom circumstances have naturally associated him, the religious congregation with which he is connected, and the community in which he lives.

It is not only religiously, but socially true that a man is "not his own." Not only municipal, but social laws justly subject every man to taxation for the common good. Every man is bound to pay tribute to society, in time, in counsel, in labor, and in money. Analogous to the loyalty which every one owes to the government, is the public spirit and the jealous concern for the public good which every member of society ought to feel. Now and then you will find men who recognize these social obligations and show their loyalty to society. There are great public improvements and valuable institutions, whose founders and supporters coming generations will rise up to bless as benefactors of society. And as you push your inquiries into the smaller circles of society, the names multiply of those who have wrought for the public good. And there are social benefits enjoyed, numerous and great, the names of whose authors are known to few, and perhaps none; but their works follow them.

There are thus some who do not live to themselves. There are some who do not ask, "Am I my brother's keeper?" There are some who remember the poor, and the unfortunate, and the sick, and the outcasts, and them that are in prison, and the orphan, and the stranger, and the homeless. There are some who consult their neighbor's feelings and interests—the common interest, and the general good.

Whence, now, come these good works

—this remembrance of others—public spirit, charity, philanthropy? As you compare Christianized with heathen and pagan lands, the answer is, for the most part, all this comes from the Bible.

What of social good, and whatever exemption from social evil we as a nation and as a community enjoy, we owe, for the most part, to the Bible. Suppose that all who profess to obey the Bible were true to its spirit, and constantly and fully obedient to all its precepts, what a community we should be! And suppose *all* were thus true to the Spirit of the Bible—those who profess and those who do not profess—how pleasant, how pure, how ennobling a social atmosphere would surround us and our children! How the intelligent and refined would seek a residence among us, to find a safe retreat for their children from the divers evils which everywhere else so disgrace the forms and poison the streams of social life!

How desirable, then, that the Bible should be the counselor of our young men—your counselor, my hearers, who are already giving character, or want of character, as the case may be, to our social life! Those who have hitherto been prominent for good, or for no good, here in social life, are passing away. You are taking their places, not merely to drink at fountains already provided, not simply to enter upon others' labors, not to be recipients only; but to affect, for good or for evil, these fountains yourselves, and to open new ones, to sow the seeds from which our children are to gather grapes or thorns, to make the social life of this community and nation better or worse.

Very likely this is more than you have engaged to do. You have not signed a contract for doing the one or the other. But this does not secure us against the evil you may do; and it does not secure to us, and to yourselves, and to the world, and to God, the good you may do, and the good you ought to do!

We want you to make the Bible your counselor, because we know that it will continually remind you of this your responsibility, and reason with you and entreat you on the one hand, and solemnly warn you on the other. We want you to make the Bible your counselor, both on your own account and on our and our children's account. When we meet you, or hear of you, in social life, whether here at home or abroad, we would be proud of you. We would have no occasion to blush for you, or to apologize for you. Once, at least, when I was away from home and traveling with a large company, I found that I had a personal interest in the reputation and character of every young man in Kalamazoo. One of them was with us. I will not say whether I had occasion to be proud or to be ashamed—but it was one of the two!

We want to find you, and every one of you, worthy of the confidence of your employers; fit companions for our daughters, and safe examples for our sons; well informed and cultivated in mind; refined in your manners, and pure in your heart and life. And we believe the Bible to be the surest guide to politeness, the best hand-book for the gentleman, the most effectual safe-guard for reputation and character. We want to see each of you a worthy member of society, taking the highest place and occupying the largest sphere to which your abilities entitle you; wise in counsel, liberal in spirit, earnestly devoted to the public good, and, for society's sake, making the most of the talents which God has committed to your keeping. For your own sake, we want you to make the Bible your counselor, as you come within the range of the temptations of social life, that you may be saved from its vices, that you may not disappoint the hopes which, to a fond mother's eyes, were like a halo around your cradled head, that you may not make a wreck of hopes which you yourself have been cherishing now for long years.

Other counselors, we know, you are liable to have—and some of them positively evil counselors, for the young man almost as certainly falls among such, as the traveler from Jerusalem to Jericho fell among thieves—and we fear for you if you do not make the Bible your chosen counselor. I cannot dwell longer on this head, for the time is passing. I had intended to give you a sample of the Bible's counsels with reference to many things included in our social life. I can now only refer you to the portion of Scripture which was read this evening, from the first and fourth chapters of the Book of Proverbs, and quote you the words of the wise man: "Rejoice, O young man, in thy

youth, and let thy heart cheer thee in the days of thy youth, and walk in the ways of thine heart and in the sight of thine eyes; but know thou that for all these things God will bring thee into judgment." "Remember now thy Creator in the days of thy youth, while the evil days come not, nor the years draw nigh, when thou shalt say, I have no pleasure in them." And the words of Paul, which I wish might be written in every young man's memorandum-book, and inscribed in letters of gold upon all the avenues of our social life—"Whatsoever things are true, whatsoever things are honest, whatsoever things are just, whatsoever things are pure, whatsoever things are lovely, whatsoever things are of good report; if there be any virtue,* and if there be any praise,† think on these things."

---

* *i. e.* Any other virtue.

† *i. e.* Whatsoever is worthy of praise.

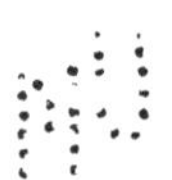

II. It is equally important, I remark, in the second place, that the young man make the Bible his counselor as he stands upon the threshold of *business* life.

This remark, I am afraid, will not be as readily assented to as the previous one. Most associate the Bible, to a greater or less extent, with *social* life. They have not forgotten the family Bible, and more or less of the language of the Bible is familiar to them, in connection with these social relations which we sustain. But it is to be feared that many, even of those who profess to make the Bible their counselor at home, have very little thought about carrying the Bible with them to their places of business. And it is to be feared that many deliberately settle the question with themselves, at the outset, that it will not do to undertake to do business according to the Bible.

To those who would leave the Bible at home, as a matter of course, who regard it as a book for the Sabbath, and a book of abstract doctrine, it needs to be said that the Bible is one of the most practical of all books, and as practical for every other day of the week as for the Sabbath; as appropriate to the shop as to the parlor, and as binding on the street and behind the counter, as in the nursery and in the Sabbath-school. And to those who have so summarily settled the question that business cannot be carried on successfully according to the principles of the Bible, it needs to be said that the Bible is no more out of place in the counting-house than it is in the dwelling-house. If there are many who have taken this position, the Bible would seem to have a special mission; and none could be more important in these days of extensive trade and commercial enterprise—to enter at once the field of business life, and proclaim in thunder tones its "Thus saith the Lord," to our business men.

The dangers to be encountered in business life are perhaps as great, and as fatal to the soul, as those of social life. The evils of the former are less demonstrative and less rapid in their destructive work; but who shall say that a corrupt conscience is not more loathsome in the sight of God, and ultimately more fatal to the individual, than corrupt social habits?

Parents often, doubtless, feel that if their sons can only be got past the unsteadiness of youth, and sobered down to regular application to business, a long agony will be over; but although to some extent this may be true, yet their sons are only surrounded by *new* dangers.

Another has described the field of business life as "a most disastrous one to human virtue. If its chronicles could be written," he says, "they would furnish as well some of the saddest as some of the brightest chapters in the annals of the race. To an eye gifted with spiritual discernment, it is a field strown with memorials of the dead, surpassing, as much in their sorrowful significance as in their numbers, the bones which have whitened the soil of Leipsic or of Waterloo. Where War has slain its thousands, Commerce has slain its tens of thousands; with other weapons indeed, but with a more terrible and far-reaching mortality. It presents to us no batteries and bayonets, no blood and carnage. It strikes not at the body, though this sometimes falls; but at the soul. It smites with a secret leprosy, which spreads its fatal virus through the arteries, even where there is every outward indication of health and happiness." Young men who stand upon the threshold of this department of life, "are breathing an infected atmosphere, and in jeopardy every hour."

If this be true, does not the young man, standing where he does, need a bold, wise, and faithful counselor — a counselor that shall be bold enough to question stereotyped rules and manners, wise enough to distinguish between apparent and real success, and show that all is not gold that glitters, and faithful enough to resist the influence of custom, and insist upon it—even though it be in the face of all the world—that a good conscience and honesty and integrity are worth more than millions of money?

When the *Henry Clay* was burned on the Hudson river ten years ago, among the number whose lives were sacrificed was Hon. STEPHEN ALLEN, an aged and opulent merchant of New York. He had been mayor of the city, and had filled various other public offices, greatly to his own credit and to the satisfaction of his fellow-citizens. When the body was recovered, there was found in his pocket-book a well-worn newspaper slip, of which the following is a copy:

"Keep good company or none.

"Never be idle.

"If your hands cannot be usefully employed, attend to the cultivation of your mind.

"Always speak the truth.

"Make few promises.

"Live up to your engagements.

"Keep your own secrets, if you have any.

"When you speak to a person, look him in the face.

"Good company and good conversation are the very sinews of virtue.

"Good character is above all things else.

"Your character cannot be essentially injured except by your own acts.

"If any one speaks evil of you, let your life be so that none will believe him.

"Drink no kind of intoxicating liquors.

"Ever live (misfortunes excepted) within your income.

"When you retire to bed, think over what you have been doing during the day.

"Make no haste to be rich, if you would prosper.

"Small and steady gains give competency, with tranquillity of mind.

"Never play at any kind of game of chance.

"Avoid temptation, lest you may not withstand it.

"Earn money before you spend it.

"Never run into debt, unless you see a way to get out again.

"Never borrow, if you can possibly avoid it.

"Do not marry until you are able to support a wife.

"Never speak evil of any one.

"Be just before you are generous.

"Keep yourself innocent, if you would be happy.

"Save when you are young, to spend when you are old.

"Read over the above maxims at least once a week."

As this was published in the newspapers in connection with his death, doubtless every one felt "that was the secret of his success." And doubtless many an employer and many a father said to himself, "Would that my young men, would that my sons, would only make these maxims their rule of life!" And, very likely, it was the feeling of many, as they after that met the gay young men of New York on Broadway, and spending their leisure hours about hotels and at places of amusement, "What a pity they are not as wise as Stephen Allen!"

And such a little counselor as his in many a man's pocket-book would be worth more to him than a fortune to start with. But what I have to say now is that if every person of good sense recognized the wisdom of that eminent merchant, and felt that they had discovered the secret of his success, what must every sensible man's response be to the proposition that the young man, as a business man, should make the Bible his counselor?

Full of wisdom as these maxims which I have just read are, some of them, after all, are somewhat defective, and the best of them are simply Scripture maxims, the language only a little varied. Now, why not supply whatever deficiency there is in these, and have them all the very best. The Bible not only includes the best of these, but many others equally appropriate and equally full of wisdom. I had hoped to be able to quote some of these, and show how luminous they are with practical wisdom, when we look at them with an eye to their application to the business affairs of life; but I have not time, and I can only add under this head, that while the Bible abounds in practical maxims which point directly towards success, it contains no requirements that are at all inconsistent with any of the true elements of success. The impression, I know, of some is that here and there it would be necessary to leave the Bible to the right or to the left, in order to be shrewd, and to maintain a reputation for business sagacity; but our text is right, and they are wrong. "Turn not from it to the right hand or to the left," and keep it for this very purpose, in order that thou mayest do wisely; "then thou shalt have good success."

III. I remark, thirdly, that the young man needs to make the Bible his counselor, as he stands on the threshold of *political* life.

You will understand that I do not mean to designate by this term "political life," that narrow, tortuous, dirty, and often underground path which the mere partisan travels, and sometimes travels on his hands and knees. I mean that broad and exalted field which stretches out before every young American, full of responsibilities and glorious in its privileges—the field of citizenship and statesmanship. Alas! that the word politics has been so prostituted as to make it seem almost of the nature of a caricature to place it side by side with the Bible, as if the two might be made to stand together without mutual repulsion! Would that the effort to keep them side by side were not left, to so great an extent as it is, to ministers of the Gospel! Would that the point here made were not so rarely found outside of the sermon! Would that what the pulpit thus preaches to young men were practised by all Christians before their eyes!

Christian citizens are not few in numbers, nor small in their influence. Christians are found among our law-makers and law pleaders; and Christians are to be found in our national and state and municipal and military officers; yet the Christian element is sadly wanting in our political life. Even high-toned morality, to say nothing of Christian principle, Christian sensitiveness, a jealousy for the honor and glory of God, a concern for the progress of Christ's kingdom—even high-toned morality seems, almost by common consent, to be almost wholly ruled out from the sphere of politics. Even in these days, when it would seem an easy thing to be a pure patriot and an honest citizen, from simple love of country, and from the simple sight of such strange spectacles, so shocking as they seem to our moral sense—spectacles of foul treason against and wholesale fraud upon the Government—even in these days, how constantly we are shocked by glaring evidence and by painful suspicions of the corruptness of our political life! How refreshing is every exhibition of pure patriotism, of political honesty and independence, of official integrity!

Here and there a Christian of eminent ability and high position, both in civil and in military life, shows us—and the exhibition thrills the hearts of even worldly men—what virtue, what strength, and what glory the religious element gives to political life. We were yesterday reminded, here upon this platform—and I was glad that the testimony came from one who did not speak as from the pulpit—reminded of WASHINGTON'S piety as the crowning excellence of the army's and nation's head.* And who has not felt

* The anniversary of the birth of Washington had been observed the day before, in the Presbyterian Church,

that the flag-officer of our gun-boats is the more of a soldier for being a Christian?*

---

when the remark alluded to was made by the Honorable CHARLES E. STUART, formerly United States Senator from Michigan, in his introduction to the reading of the Farewell Address.

* The speaker here referred in glowing terms to the Christian character of Gen. McCLELLAN, and to the language which the telegraph had just attributed to Gen. BURNSIDE, implying his unwavering faith in God, amid the disasters and delays which accompanied the early movements of the great expedition called by his name. Upon the repetition of the sermon, Mr. HUGGINS added the following:—

"I am thankful that the past week has furnished me another name from among the officers and statesmen on whom our country is especially relying in this the hour of her trial—another name to enforce the point which I am making here, viz., that the Bible should be the young man's counselor in political life. Says Secretary STANTON: 'Much has recently been said of military combinations and *organizing* victory. I hear such phrases with apprehension. They commenced in infidel France, with the Italian campaign, and resulted in Waterloo. Who can organize victory? Who can combine the elements of success on the battle field? We owe our recent victories to the Spirit of the Lord, that moved our soldiers to rush into battle, and filled the hearts of our enemies with terror and dismay. The inspiration that conquered

Did the Bible make FRANKLIN any the less a statesman? or WILBERFORCE? In the closing days of JACKSON and of CLAY, did the Bible on their tables and in their hands — their acknowledged counselor then — dim the lustre of their political renown?

The time is passing, and I must hasten to a conclusion. But I have said enough to enforce the point that our young men, as they stand upon the threshold of political life, need to make the Bible their counselor — for their own sake, for our country's sake, and for the whole world's sake — for the whole world is becoming more and more interested, and vitally interested, in the questions of American politics, and in the character of American citizenship.

---

in battle was from on high; and wherever there is the same inspiration, there will be the same results.'

"It would seem that Mr. STANTON, when he gathered his books and counselors about him in his youth, did not leave the Bible out."

IV. I remark, in the fourth place, that the young man needs to make the Bible his counselor, as he stands upon the threshold of an *endless* life.

Upon this point I need not dwell in order to enforce it. The very mention of it, side by side with these limited spheres of life, is enough to startle one! It is as if we heard the echo of our footfall sounding out from the solemn spaces of eternity!

Standing, though a young man seems especially to do, in contact only with those more apparent and apparently more pressing realities, it is really upon the threshold of an endless life. Looking out now upon this, shall he take counsel of his own wayward and wicked heart—of a vain, deceitful world? Where shall he find a counselor, as he stands here—and here he is all the time standing—except in the Bible, which solemnly warns him of hell and points him to heaven?

III.

THE DANGER FROM EVIL COMPANIONS.

PREACHED SABBATH EVENING, MARCH 9, 1862.*

PROVERBS i. 10, 15; AND iv. 15.

"MY SON, IF SINNERS ENTICE THEE, CONSENT THOU NOT. WALK NOT THOU IN THE WAY WITH THEM; REFRAIN THY FOOT FROM THEIR PATH. AVOID IT, PASS NOT BY IT, TURN FROM IT, AND PASS AWAY."

WE were made social beings. He who made us said, "It is not good that man should be alone." These words point not to wedded life only, but also to the com-

---

* This was the last sermon written and preached by the lamented Pastor. Early in the week following its preparation, he was seized with the disease which terminated his life, and he expired the second Sabbath after its delivery.

panionships and friendships of childhood and youth. If we have a pleasant thought, or experience a feeling of pleasure, we are the happier—or we were made to be—for sharing it with others. "Two," the wise man says, "are better than one; for if they fall, the one will lift up his fellow; but woe to him that is alone when he falleth. And if one prevail against him, two shall withstand him; and a three-fold cord is not quickly broken."

And yet, alas! beautiful as is childhood when we see it hand in hand, and beautiful and helpful as the friendships of youth often are, how often has this fountain of happiness and help, which was opened in Eden, proved a source only of evil! Two have often proved worse than one. Instead of "the one lifting up," it has been the one dragging down "his fellow." If you are just ready to slip upon the ice, it does not help you to have another, who is already going, seize you by the hand. If two take each other by the hand, going in opposite directions—the one down hill, and the other struggling to get up—the chances are as nine to one that they will go together; and I need not say in which direction! So in these companionships of life, the advantage is generally, if the evil and the good are linked together, on the side of the evil. As moral beings we are all, indeed, subject to strong downward tendencies; but, to a greater or less extent, in various ways, these are counteracted in the case of most, so that the great majority, as they start out in active life, are not standing on the steepest and most slippery places; and so long as they are not, we have hope that the grace of God may intervene to overcome these downward tendencies, to displace the gravitating principle, and to lift them upward, as they struggle up the steep ascent of virtue. The steep descents, and slippery places, however, are not far off, and the shortest road to them lies through *evil companionship*. If another reaches out his hand to us, we had better look well to his footing. It may be safe for us to go alone; and yet he may help us.

Thus it is not good to be alone; and yet it is often worse to be in company, our companions being what they are. And hence, next in importance to the question, who and what our parents are—they who start us on the journey of life—is the question who and what our companions are. For companions or associates we shall certainly have, from our childhood up, and we are perpetually surrounded and followed by influences from this source, either for good or for evil; and we know that in a world like this, the evil influences far outnumber the good. The evil influences from this source lurk at every door, to corrupt the children of the household as they pass out. They lie along every path to meet them, in whatever direction they go. They await the young man on the street, at his place of business, and at every point where he comes in contact with his fellows. No pains of parents or employees, and no pains of his own, can wholly prevent his exposure to them.

And yet it is not just as if he were breathing an infected atmosphere, or were exposed to contagious disease; for, as moral beings, we are not mere passive recipients. Contact with evil does not necessarily injure us. (It does if we consent to it, and needlessly suffer it.) Mere exposure is not necessarily fatal. Our character, and our moral condition and destiny, are in our own hands. The injunction, "Resist the devil, and he will flee from you," shows that we have the power to resist; and the solemn warnings and imperative commands of our text show that evil and its agents are not our masters, except by our own consent. It may seem to parents and guardians, as they look out upon the evil influences which lurk in the early companionships of life, that they are fearfully powerful, and that the ability to resist them is weak and unreliable; yet there can be no mistake as to the fact of the responsibility which lies at the door of every moral being, old or young. The parent recognizes it, as he commands and entreats his son to be on his guard, to be careful what company he keeps, and to take care of himself, looking to God for help. The son and the daughter recognize it, as they reply, "You need not be anxious on our account; we are not afraid; we are able to take care of ourselves."

But now the next question is, will they take care of themselves? Looking to God for help, will they resist the devil, and the agents and instrumentalities which the devil employs? This is a question of fearful interest. Parents ask it with aching hearts and trembling apprehension. Employers tell us they are almost afraid to ask it; it awakens so little hope and so much apprehension. He who is called to preach God's Word, asks it with anxious concern, knowing that his voice will be likely to have little power, whether in the way of admonition or entreaty, if evil companions have the ear of those to whom he preaches.

My object to-night, as you see, is to call the attention, especially of young men, to the importance of the question what company they keep, and particularly to the dangers of evil companionship. Perhaps I have said enough already as to the fact of danger from this source; and yet I fear that this is the point of greatest danger, that the danger is not sufficiently seen and felt. Let me, therefore, tell you, young men, directly, and in so many words, that there is danger, and of the most fearful kind, in these companionships which you form, or which you suffer others to form—you, as one of the parties, simply consenting thereto. Would that I could sound this out so loud and long that it would ring in your ears wherever you go, and be a warning voice under just the circumstances when you most need to be warned.

Warnings in the house of God, I suppose, seem very much a matter of course. Would, not that the preacher's voice, but that this Word of God which he preaches, would ring in your ears on the corners of the streets, at the doors of these bar-rooms and ball-rooms and saloons, and in whatever rooms or wherever else *sinners entice you.* "Walk not thou in the way with them; refrain thy foot from their path. Avoid it, pass not by it, turn from it, and pass away!" "He that walketh with wise men shall be wise; but a companion of fools"—the wicked are not only wicked, but fools in the sight of God—

"a companion of fools shall be destroyed!"

I might put you on your guard more particularly against many sins and dangers to which you are exposed—against profanity, dishonesty, intemperance, gambling, licentiousness; but in this word of warning to-night, a multitude of dangers are summed up in one. Escape this, and you escape them. Pay no heed to this warning, and it were almost useless to warn you further.

Suppose I were to approach you, surrounded in a bar-room by a company of gay companions, or in some retired room where the cards were on the table, and you made just the number for the game, and that I were to undertake to put you on your guard against the dangers which I should see gathering their snaky folds about you! No matter with what skill I should seek to accomplish my object—even though I could summon from the dead, as Samuel's shrouded form arose before the terror-stricken Saul, the face and form of some dear departed friend—a sainted mother or sister—should I be likely to succeed under such circumstances? Would you be likely to turn your back upon that gay company, just as the invitation went round to drink? Suppose you should say, "No" once! Would you not have to say it twice and thrice; and would you be likely to hold out a great while, one against half a dozen? Would you not be likely to say to yourself, caught in the snare of an easily-deceived and deceiving heart, "The easier way, after all, will be to drink this once, and say no more about it?" And, by the way, "this once"—what a key "this once" has been to transgressions and their consequences, whose name is "legion!"

"'Did you ever attend the theatre?' said a young man to a blue-eyed maiden, who hung on his arm as they promenaded the streets of New York, one mild evening in October. The cheek of the lady crimsoned with a blush as she answered the interrogatory in the negative, and added: 'My mother has taught me from childhood that it was wrong to attend such places.' 'But your mother formed perhaps improper prejudices, from exaggerated accounts given by others; for I have often heard her say she never attended one in her life.' And he spoke eloquently of the drama, tragedy and comedy; and dwelt with pathos on the important lessons which we there learn of human nature. 'Go with me once,' said he, 'and judge for yourself.' Persuasion and curiosity triumphed over the maternal precept and example, as she hesitatingly replied, 'I'll go but once.' She went, and in that theatre a charm came over her like the one which the serpent sent forth from his dove-like eye. She went again and again, and from that house of mirth and laughter, she was led to one from the portals of which she never returned.

"Around a centre-table, where an astral lamp was shedding its mild light, sat three young ladies, while one held in her hand a pack of cards. At the back of her chair stood a young gentleman, who for years had successfully resisted every effort made by his companions to induce him to learn the characters on cards. 'Come,' said she, 'we need one to make our game; play us once, if you never play again.' Her eye, cheek, and lip, conspired to form an eloquent battery which sent forth its attacks upon the fortress of good resolutions, in which he had long stood secured, until it fell like the walls of an ancient city, when jarred by the fearful battering-ram. He learned the cards and played. A few weeks afterwards, I was passing his room at a late hour, and a candle was shedding its dim light through the window. Since that time I have looked from my chamber nearly every hour of the night, 'from close of day till morn,' and seen that light faintly struggling through the curtains that screened the inmates of that room from every eye save His which seeth alike in darkness and at noonday. Gaming brought with it disease, and death came just as he had numbered the half of three-score years and ten. During his last hours I was sitting by his bedside, when he fixed on me a look which I shall never forget, and bade me listen to his dying words. 'I might have been a different man from what I am, but it is too late now. I am convinced that there is a state of existence beyond the grave; and when I think of the retribution which awaits me in another world, I feel a horror which language is inadequate to describe.' These were among the last words he ever uttered."

But to return. The question which I ask is, would my warning, under the circumstances which I have supposed, be very likely to succeed? Had I not better warn you, and had you not better warn yourself, before you cross the threshold, and before you join the company whose steps are likely to be turned in that direction?

I point you, therefore, to-night, to the danger you are in from *evil companionships.*

And isn't there danger? Do you not see it yourself? Look at that young man.

whom you remember as a boy—his eye clear, his cheek with the hue of health upon it, his dress neat, and his whole appearance interesting and promising—but, as you meet him now, his eye is watery and restless, his face is bloated, he walks no longer with the elastic step of earlier days; all pride in regard to personal appearance is gone, or a little of it still remaining; he will not meet your eye, but looks the other way. Have you not often wished that he would not keep the company he does? Have you not felt that the set he goes with are destroying him? Is it not often said of him, that evil companions have been his ruin?

Some months ago I used to meet every day a young man whose personal appearance attracted my attention. He was particularly well dressed, and his step and all his movements indicated good habits, energy, and ambition and hope. Perhaps I had seen him before, and now observed an evident "looking up" in point of character and purpose. After a while I noticed that a change had come over him; and now there is a total contrast with his appearance then. Neatness of personal appearance, and elasticity of step and movement, are all gone. There is no ambition now, and apparently little hope; and "bad habits" seem to be written upon his face and form. I saw him one morning the past week, coming out of the back door of a saloon. I found myself silently asking the question, whether he probably found his way into the saloon for the first time *alone*.

But look into your own hearts, young men. Do you not find there danger enough to make you tremble, as from time to time you find how weak you are against the evil suggestions which come from within? With all the counteracting influences of home, and more or less of ambition to make something of yourself, the struggle you have often found a hard one, with these temptations of the heart.

Isn't it, now, almost suicidal to cast yourself away, or to suffer yourself to be surrounded by those whose habits are loose, whose lives are aimless, and whose associations, to say the least, are questionable?

If one stream, subject as it is to sudden freshets, is liable to carry away bridge and dam and mill, is it not madness in him whose property it puts in jeopardy, to suffer others above him to turn other streams into it, if he can prevent them?

It is enough to have to resist ourselves. And is he not a fool, both in the Scriptural sense and in the ordinary sense of the term, who needlessly, and with eyes open, adds foes without to foes within? And I do not use this term "foe" merely in a figurative sense; for the danger is not simply from contact with evil, and from exposure to bad example. There is often a strange disposition, and a fiendish purpose on the part of those who are already on the downward road, to get an influence over the new-comer, in order to drag him down too. And how cunningly they play their game! How well they know the weak points of their coveted prey! How stealthily they weave the net around him; or, if he resist, how mercilessly they ply the weapons of their hellish warfare. How easy to make him think that he knows better than his parents, or to shame him out of his deference to their opinions and wishes; and to set him against his employers, if they are faithful to keep a watchful eye upon him, and to prejudice him against the minister of the gospel, and the Sabbath-school, and religion; and to break up his habit of reading the Bible, and of going regularly to church! How expert they are in quoting—and, alas! what occasion is given them for it!—in quoting what church-members do, and what they do not do; and, if facts are not readily found, how easy to make them to suit their purpose!

It is the nature of the sinner not only to sin, but, in the language of the text, to "entice" others to sin. And hence, the injunction is not only "consent thou not," as if it were of little use to say that, and say nothing more, but, "my son, walk not thou in the way with them; refrain thy foot from their path;" and then, with a remarkable repetition of warning and entreaty, to give intensity to it, "avoid their path, pass not by it, turn from it, and pass away!"

But even if there were no such fearful danger of being corrupted by companionship with the reckless, and the unprincipled, and the impure, how great the injustice which a young man does himself, and how miserable the policy, to say the least, if he suffers himself to be seen and identified with such associates!

"People will, in a great degree," says another, "and not without reason, form their opinion of you upon that which they have of your friends; and there is a Spanish proverb, which says very justly, 'Tell me with whom you live, and I will tell you who you are.'"

It will not do to say that you do not care what others think, nor to place yourself in this attitude, because their opinions may happen to be incorrect; that you are not dependent upon others' opinions; and that it is enough if you take care of yourself and escape, as you expect to, the evils which are apprehended from this source.

You are dependent upon others' opinions! Is it of no consequence to you that your employer begins to suspect your honesty, because of the company you keep? May it not make some difference with you, what the merchant over the way thinks of you? Circumstances may throw you out of your situation, or he may have a more lucrative one which he wishes to fill.

You are not independent of the good opinion of men whose names you do not know. Suppose some one abroad writes to one of these men: "My attention has been called to such a young man in your community, as a competent, or a promising business man. Please write me what you think of him, and especially what you know of his habits and associations." Can you not conceive of circumstances which would make it very fortunate for you, if the answer should be entirely favorable? But what if it were this: "I am not personally acquainted with the young man in regard to whom you inquire, and I do not know any thing against him, except that I have frequently seen him of late standing idly about our hotels, and often in company with young men whose reputation is not very good?" Would not that be very likely to close the correspondence?

But it is time for me to ask a question

which I wish to ask, in view of this great danger to which all young men are exposed.

My question is this—What do you, my friends, in view of this danger, propose to do?

There are, doubtless, multitudes of young men in the land who never have asked themselves this question. They take no thought either for the morrow or for the day itself, so far as good and evil, right and wrong, as such, are concerned. They take things as they come, and as they affect the pocket, and the conveniences and pleasures of the passing hour. Apparently they have no other personal interests to look after. Reputation and character they have little thought about. To make money, and have something good to eat and drink, and to enjoy themselves, seem their only aims.

There are others who have thoughts about these things, but they are reckless;

they "don't care," particularly if you wish them to care. If pressed with the question, "What they propose to do?" they do not propose to do any thing. This, at least, is the language of their looks and actions. If I am addressing any such, let me ask you what right, my friends, you have to be reckless—to assume this "don't-care" attitude? Sometimes it is, "Nobody cares for me, and I care for nobody;" and again, in an uncharitable mood, you resent the care which is manifested for you. Others *do* care for you, and you are bound to care for yourself and for them. A want of good sense in such things we can tolerate in a boy, hoping he will grow wiser as he grows older; but a young man ought to be above all real or assumed indifference to the good opinions of others and of his own interests.

But there are many who have felt the importance of this question, and they have given it more or less consideration. They do not mean to go with the worst of those whom they may come in contact with; and yet they feel as if they must be on good and familiar terms with most of those into whose company they may fall. It is very pleasant to be popular, or, at least, to be in good favor with those who are. Hence they make up their minds to avoid the worst companions; but they do not propose to be very particular. They mean to have their eyes about them, and they feel a little pride in their conscious ability to take care of themselves. What they propose to do is to secure the end, without being troubled about the means. They propose to avoid being ruined, as a great many, they admit, have been.

Conceive of one in a little boat on Niagara river, who hasn't made up his mind how far down the river he will sail before he will stop. But he understands what an awful thing it would be to go over the falls; he trembles when he thinks of it;

he is determined that he will not be caught down where the waters make that fearful plunge. Meanwhile, his hand is on the oar, and he floats along. The waters give an ominous leap now and then, but he only grasps his oar the tighter, and determines that he will be on his guard, and still floats on. He is warned from the shore, and the warning startles him a little; but he thinks it unmanly to seem to be afraid, and still floats on. As he did not propose to do any thing but to resolve that he would not be caught as others had been; so he does nothing but re-resolve. But he is in the rapids, and now—what? You may not see, but you know the end!

Young men! the current of Niagara is not the only dangerous current. There are leaping waves and boiling eddies, and a mighty under-tow, equally resistless, and more fatal than any you see there. It will not do simply to determine that you will avoid the worst companions. but not be very particular whither you float, and where you are found, and what you are about!

My advice to you would be, if you will hear me—though do not follow it, if it is not wise counsel—my advice would be this:

I. And first—and in this remark let me suppose that you are a new comer, a stranger among strangers, or just entering upon early manhood, and as yet with no intimate associates—make up your mind, *settle it* with yourself, that to have no companions is better than to have such as are of dangerous or doubtful character. I have not forgotten the thought we started with, that "it is not good to be alone." I know what a young man's social nature is. I remember that I said that almost inevitably we shall have associates; but upon new ground you may certainly take a little time to look about you. It is not necessary that you offer yourself at once as a candidate for companionships, or that you open your arms and give an unrestricted ear to all who may approach you. There will be very little embarrassment in pursuing this course; and you can easily bear the self-denial of going your own way, and keeping your own counsel for a while, if you will only give this matter a little consideration in advance, and give yourself to understand that it is a matter legitimately under your own control, and one in which a little caution will be as much in place as in the choice of your business, or the selection of a boarding-place.

Make up your mind, then, to have no companions until you can find such as you have good reason to believe will prove safe ones. In the meantime, you need not give any occasion for unkind feelings towards you, or for any reasonable objections to the course which you pursue.

You can be a gentleman to all you come in contact with. You need not seem proud nor exclusive. You simply hold yourself somewhat in reserve. So long as you do this, you are easily your own master. Within these reserved limits it is comparatively easy to resist the approaches of temptation, and to say, "No!" To do this is a very different thing, if one has rushed heedlessly into company, and at the outset let down all the bars of self-respect and reserve. This is to ignore the fact that there is danger; or, knowing it, and seeing it, it is weakly and cowardly to surrender in advance.

II. Again, not only in the meantime look well about you, but *take a long look ahead;* and I will add another thing to this, frequently look back also.

The plans and expectations of youth naturally bring the future more or less into view; but, nevertheless, I think that the young man's eye, especially when he is forming his first companionships, is very largely filled by the present. There is so much that is novel and attractive and exciting in the scenes upon which he enters, that he is liable to think and feel and act as if these days were to last always, and to lose sight of the weightier responsibilities and more important interests which will be upon his hands a few years later. Hence, I say, take a long look ahead, and see the bearing this question of associates has upon those grave responsibilities and important interests in which the happiness and usefulness of your life are involved.

I say, also, *frequently look back*, because in that direction lie the innocent days of your childhood, which it will do you good to look back upon, and the sweet associations of home, and fond memories of father and mother, and brothers and sisters. A look in that direction will remind you of what you owe to yourself, to your truer and better self; and what you owe to your parents and to your family, and to the place which gave you birth.

III. Again, it will help you in this matter of controlling your companionships *to attend closely to your business.*

There are other motives for doing this; but this also is a motive, that it will be a safeguard to you against dangerous associates. It will be an excuse for saying, "No," and for going the other way—an excuse which none can gainsay—your business, which requires your attention, and your obligations to your employers; for do not fail to keep these in mind as an honest man, and be brave and manly enough not to be ashamed to have this known.

IV. Again, be sure and have some safe retreat from the social evils to which you are exposed.

It will be fortunate, though you, perhaps, may not think so, if you are not out of reach of your home. But if away from home, have some place which will seem at least a little like home—a room of your own, if you can command one; and the more it is out of the way the better—and make it as pleasant as you can. Invite yourself thither by all the attractions with which you can fill it—though they need not be many nor expensive—but be careful whom else you invite. And here, so far as you can command the time for it, make books your companions. A very little caution will make them safe, pleasant, and profitable companions. They will never invite you, and almost force you, to drink, when you do not wish to; and, if you will make it a rule never to have one in your room which you would be ashamed to have your father or mother or sister see, they will never corrupt you.

With such a castle of your own, and

with such pleasant and profitable friends within its walls, and your careful, deliberate choice of outsiders to meet you there in your leisure hours, and such social intercourse as you may easily have with intelligent families, it would seem that you would be in comparatively little danger from this great evil of which I have been speaking.

V. Again, I would suggest—and if you are really disposed in self-defence to guard against this great evil, I think you will see that the suggestion is a practical suggestion—that you connect yourself with some Christian congregation, and with the Bible Class in the Sabbath-school.

It is hardly necessary that I address you separately who are not new comers, and who may be already to a greater or less extent involved in the net-work of evils which spring from this prolific source. What is appropriate to any one case, will apply substantially to all cases. The difficulties are greater in your case than in that of the new comer; but only make these principles and this policy your own, and quit yourselves like men, and you may yet escape the perils that surround you.

VI. But my counsel would be incomplete without one more suggestion—and it is the most important of all—*make Christ your friend and companion.**

---

* As the pen here dropped from the failing grasp of the dying Pastor, it appears to have rapidly traced the words, "He, a young man," referring to Christ, the topic of the last head—which in the pulpit he developed eloquently, and at some length. There are one or two blank spaces in the last few pages of the manuscript, indicating an intention to commit further thoughts to paper, which his departing strength or the pressure of other duties prevented.

THE END.

www.ingramcontent.com/pod-product-compliance
Lightning Source LLC
LaVergne TN
LVHW021410110826
845150LV00007B/1862

* 9 7 8 1 4 2 5 5 1 1 3 4 0 *